ZAZEN

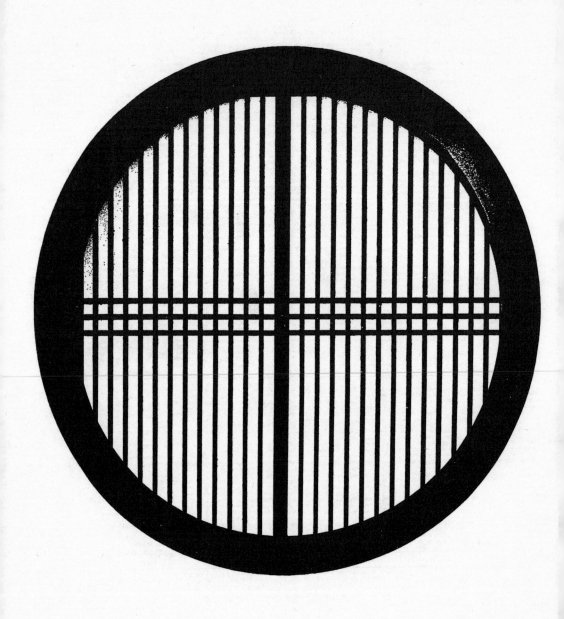

Else Madelon Hooykaas photos and diary
Bert Schierbeek essay

ZAZEN

Omen Press, Tucson, Arizona

Translation by
Charles McGeehan

© 1971 Uitgeverij N.Kluwer nv
Deventer, Netherlands

1974 paperback edition
ISBN 0-912358-41-6
By Permission.

Photography is
the art of not looking for It.
An art of waiting.
The art of letting It come to us.

Robert Leverant: Zen in the art of photography

Bibliography

R.B.Blackney:	The way of life (Mentor Books, New York)
R.H.Blyth:	Haiku (The Hokuseido Press, Tokyo)
Horst Hammitzsch:	Chardo, der Teeweg (Otto Wilhelm Barth Verlag, Munchen-Planegg)
Eugen Herrigel:	Zen in de kunst van het boogshieten (De Driehoek, Amsterdam)
Gusty L.Herrigel:	Der Blumenweg (Otto Wilhelm Barth Verlag, Munchen-Planegg)
Lautze:	Tau Teh Tsjing (o.a. N. Kluwer, Deventer)
Paul Reps:	Zenzin-zenonzin (N. Kluwer, Deventer)
Bert Schierbeek	De tuinen van Zen (De Bezige Bij, Amsterdam)
Lucien Stryk & Takashi Ikemoto:	Zen Poems, Prayers, Sermons, Anecdotes, Interviews (Doubleday & Co., New York)
Ingeborg Y.Wendt:	Zen, Japan und der Westen (Paul List Verlag, Munchen)
Peter Weber Schafer:	Zen. Ausspruche und Verse der Zen Meister gesammelt (Insel Verlag)

A Zen priest sees a young monk, who is seated before the image of Buddha, reciting sutras. He asks him:
"What are you doing there?"
"I want to become a Buddha (an Enlightened One)."
The priest picks up a stone, goes to sit next to him, and starts to rub the stone intensively with his hand.
The monk looks on for a short while and asks:
"What are you doing?"
The Zen master answers: "I want to rub this stone for as long as it takes it to become a mirror."
"At that you'll never succeed."
"Exactly; nor will you ever become a Buddha by merely sitting and reciting sutras."
The same Zen master could also have chased him out of the temple with the words:
"Have you washed your dish yet? No? Then do that first."
This Zen master was to be surprised one evening by the visit of one of his pupils, while he was sitting in the lotus posture before his wooden image of Buddha and reciting sutras.
"But Master, you tell us that by sitting and reciting we'd never attain Enlightenment and at-Oneness, and yet you're doing it yourself."
"Well, as old as I am, I'm used to it by now," answers the master.
The pupil went away unsatisfied, but returned the next day. And what to his dismay does he see? The master is with an ax chopping up the wooden Buddha figure and dashing it into the fire.
"But Master, what are you doing now?"
"Today I'm cold," answered the master.
One says that this pupil, by way of this answer, which illuminated his mind like a flash of lightning, obtained the insight that in Zen terms is called Satori.

The founder of Zen Buddhism, Bodhidharma, arrived in China in the sixth century from India. He was invited to meet the then Emperor, Wu, who was himself a Buddhist. The first thing that the emperor asked him was:

"What is the most important principle of Buddhism?"
"The absolute vacuum, the absolute void," was the reply.
"Then who is now standing before me?" asked the emperor.
"I wouldn't be able to tell you," answered Bodhidharma.

What is Zen?
Zen comes from the Chinese word Ch'an, which is a
corruption of the Sanskrit Dhyana, for 'contemplation' or
'meditation'. In far Eastern Buddhism, the different forms
taken by meditation became one of the grounds on which
the various sects were formed. If until Bodhidharma's
patriarchy in India, Mahayana, the most evolved and
extensive form of Buddhism, was a School of Gradual
Awakening, the new Mahayana teaching he introduced in
the Far East could be called the School of Sudden
Awakening. The succeeding generations of Far Eastern
masters who were to follow up on his teachings did so by
using anecdotes, koans, or quick question-answer games
called mondos. He himself summed up his method as
follows:
A special transmission which works outside the scriptures.
Independent of words or letters.
Direct focus on the soul.
Getting insight into oneself.
A dynamic form of meditation to break through the
'gradual' form.
Zen won't wait seven long lives for Nirvana; Zen wants
Nirvana Now.
The koans and mondos are indicators, forefingers that point
at the moon, without being the moon itself.

Zen is impatient; the Zen Buddhists are the rebels of
Buddhism, yet they can and do refer to Buddha, who,
preaching, once said nothing, holding up a flower for his
audience to see. None of those present understood this
gesture, except Mahakasyapa, who began to smile. And
Buddha then said to him:
"This is the lore of the True Symbol, which is non-symbolic,

a doctrine without words, outside the limits of tradition and
a direct way to Nirvana."
So the sign of verity that signifies nothing is Zen teaching:
Be without symbols, unsignified, without prejudice or
preconception, be open, be empty.
"Don't expect the gods to help you," said Buddha, "they
are born under the same laws of cause and effect as you, the
laws of Karma. They cannot do anything to alter their part
of fortune. Everything, or all that you can expect, is what
comes solely from yourself. Bear in mind: Each of you can
attain to this higher power."
Herein one sees the clear distinction between Christianity
and Buddhism. Buddhism knows of no personal godhead
one can refer to. One must refer to one's self and *can;* for
the Buddha abides and lives in every human being and
everyone is equipped to become a Buddha.
Break out of the harness of fixed notions and illusory
preconceptions within which you were brought up; become
the cork upon life's bottle. If you've been able to pop the
cork, then go stand naked and without sureties before the
mirror and see who you are.
Smash up the mirror and step through it, a Zen master
would say.
Smash up the 'God-I' dichotomy, abandon such binary
conceptions as yes/no, good or bad, high or low. Believe in
the basic vacuity of any idea or conception whatsoever, so
as to become 'fully-empty'—that is, fully conscious in the
void of a clear mental space—thus complete.

To speak in accord with a Christian mystic, Meister
Eckhart: "God was empty when he created the world, and
he created us in his image."
In other words the Formless is the source of all forms in
which we live, which we undergo as opposites, couterparts,
correspondences or comparisons. They have a single
common denominator—the vacuum, the void which is
'fully-empty', vacant and thereby creative, i.e., open.
Under this denominator one is still unborn and still not

'signified', nor is one yet given 'meaning' or 'sense'.
One could call the content of Buddha's Teaching a
'Reversion to one's Pre-Birth Face.' And the man who
succeeds at this and thus is standing on the threshold of
Nirvana, but returns and mingles among his pupils so as to
teach them the way thereto, and supports them with his
experience, one calls a Bodhisattva. Before birth there was
no suffering, one was still at-One with the Wholeness, the
integrity of things, still imbedded in and not a separate part
of Reality, of the All, or however one wants to call Nirvana.
Thus one must be reborn in this life, so as to let subject
and object converge again, a flowing together into that
region where distinctions don't exist. Zen Buddhism has
developed its own unique technique for that purpose:
Sudden Awakening. Zen wants and is Nirvana Now.

When Bodhidharma came into China and in his way wanted
to broadcast the seeds of Buddha's teaching, he came upon
fertile cultural soil in the teaching of Lao Tze, in the
wisdom of Confucius and of many other Chinese sages. But
also the practical and down-to-earth institutions of Chinese
life in general must have been exceedingly welcome to this
freebooter. Legend has it that he looked wild and unruly,
with a great beard and wide-open eyes which twinkled with
humor and sarcasm. Once he must have fallen asleep while
he was meditating; he then got so angry that he cut off
his eyelids. When they fell onto the ground the first
tea-plant arose there. And sitting quietly at drinking tea has
always been a form of meditation in Zen. Tea would keep
you awake. It is said also that he once sat so long in
meditation that his legs dropped off. There are still little
roly-poly legless figurines of him around, heavy on the
underside and lighter on topside, that you can knock over,
though always they stand up again. A little poem about this
says:

> So goes life
> Seven fallings down
> Eight times on your feet again.

Bodhidharma lived up in the mountains for years. One day
a man arrived in front of his hut to speak with him, and
sat there. Bodhidharma did not open the door. He let the
man sit there for seven days: Desperate by the seventh day,
the man cut off his left arm. This bloody earnestness did
convince Bodhidharma and he asked the man, named
Hui-ko, what he wanted.
"My soul knows no rest; please put it at peace."
"Pick it up and bring it here," was the answer.
"But when I look it escapes my grasp."
"Then I've put your soul at peace."
One says that Hui-ko then attained Satori, and also that he
was further initiated by Bodhidharma to become his
successor, which happened. The master himself was to have
left China at a ripe old age to die in his birthland, India.
He died in a way worthy of a Zen Buddhist, that is, with
one sandal on a foot and the other upon his head, as one
says, roaring with laughter.
This liberating laugh shall always be a resounding presence
in Zen. It is a kind of humor grounded upon a paradox:
Being and not-being. The paradox is creative, because it
connects ideas and propositions, which normally are
experienced by reasoning as opposites. In Zen the paradox
is handled as *the medium* of approach to being. The goal is
always at-Oneness with Reality, with the 'full-void'.

One could even say: Whoever interprets dies. For he divides
what is One.
Thus the question: What's the right word? gets answered
with: You make two out of it. The little word 'right'
presupposes all-too-much, namely: *not*-right.

Each of the Zen patriarchs had his own highly original way
of choosing his successor. One day Hung-jen, the Fifth
Patriarch, was visited by a man from Kwangtung—a southern
province—who called himself Wei-lang. He said: "I have
traveled a long way and I come here to become a Buddha."
"Kwangtung? So, you are a barbarian. You can neither read
nor write? How will you ever become a Buddha?"

"Even though people are living in both North and South, the way the wind blows has no influence on their Buddha-nature. A barbarian differs from you bodily, but no more than that." At this point the master pointed to the kitchen: "Enough, now go and wash the dishes."

"This kid is too bright for his own good," he must have thought.

But when he felt the time had come to arrange for his succession, he put up notice of a contest. Whoever could compose the best verse was to succeed him. Shin-shau, his best student, wrote:

> Our body is the Bodhi-tree (whereunder Buddha
>   attained the Insight)
> Our mind a gleaming mirror
> Carefully we wipe away at it hour by hour
> So no dust can gather on it.

But he didn't win, for out of the stable came another poem:

> There is no Bodhi-tree
> Nor a clear, clean mirror
> As everything is empty
> Where then is dust to land?

This was Wei-lang's poem and he became the successor. Shin-shau hadn't stepped through the mirror: Wei-lang had indeed, even though, as legend has it, he could neither read nor write. Wei-lang, who later was to be called Hui-neng, was the second founder of Zen Buddhism. He was in the true sense 'mindless'.

The true mind is 'no-mind'; you can't use the mind to make *more* mind out of it, for that's no way to get it empty.

One could say that one thought draws out the other, but this doesn't make things any clearer, and Zen will keep on having the one thought drawn forth from the other, anyway, to make this 'void' evident and to achieve it.

Through part and counterpart unto totality.

Wei-lang was the last patriarch of Zen Buddhism. His main sermons were recorded and became *The Sutra of Wei Lang,*

the only sutra written in Chinese. He refined the technique
of the koan to the utmost. His method was grounded upon
question and counter-question and the denial of both. In
this manner he pushed the *forms* of consciousness back into
the vacuum wherefrom they arose and are indescribable.
He transmitted his teaching to five disciples, each of whom
in his own way attended to the dissemination of Zen. Huai
Jeng and Hsing Szu were the founders of the Rinzai and Soto
schools, which are still thriving in present-day Japan. Zen
fanned out across all of China. Everywhere monasteries
were springing up, with their Zendos—meditation-halls in
which Zazen, *sitting quiet and doing nothing,* was practiced.
At that time this form of meditation consisted mainly of
invoking the name of Buddha, such constant repetition of
the name of Buddha that one becomes 'empty' and then
Buddha doesn't even exist anymore.

As Saichi sang it: When I pronounce the name
                  my thoughts and troubles melt away
                  as snow thaws under the sun
                  of springtime.

From China Zen diffused through and via Korea into Japan,
where it soon took root and grew to full flower and has
maintained itself up to today. All forms of life and culture
were influenced by Zen. Zen permeated Japan like
leavening: a refreshing breeze, a whirlwind, a 'twister'.
The Zen masters were great 'nose twisters' of the assumed
and accepted realities; not only in religion, but also in all
forms of art. It took hold of people where they thought
they had firm footing, put them through a few turns at the
'zero-point' of existence and said to them: See? that's you!
By so doing, in this creation of uncertainties, it released a
chain-reaction of creative deeds. As Rinzai has said:

Sometimes I remove the man, but not the surroundings
Sometimes I remove the surroundings, but not the man
Sometimes both
Sometimes neither

The Zen monks are known as 'cloud and water people' because they drift like clouds and stream like water. Thus and so driven, they float and flow like clouds and water into all the crevices of life. Zen wouldn't leave anything as it was or 'settled', it was always in motion. The Japanese *sumi-e* painters made use of an ink mixed with glue so they'd have to fix the moment of insight in one quick brushstroke. Impossible to do over.

The *haiku* is a poem of 17 syllables, a brief form of verse in which 'the golden surface-skin of things' is recorded.

Like this one: The drunken monkey
               folds its arms over its head
               and sleeps—samadhi!

These are two areas, but also archery, the arranging of flowers, serving of tea, the laying out of gardens, sword-fighting, were turned into 'forms of meditation', into 'the Way' via which one could attain to Nirvana. A swordsman had to let his sword fly so swiftly through throat and neck of his opponent that the latter still had to shake his head before it fell off. The actor in the Japanese Noh play doesn't sing out of his throat, but his voice comes from his belly, wherein dwells his soul, which he 'empties' while singing. There was no form of life that wasn't acted upon by the 'non-form' to come out at-once with a 'new face'. And if you were to ask Huang Po "What is Buddha" you could get slapped in the face, or he'd start to roar like a lion, or to bark like a dog, "Wu, wu," which in Chinese also means, "No, no." To the question of whether a dog can partake of Buddha-nature, he also barked, "Wu, wu."
"What is Nirvana?"
"What would you answer if you were hanging by your teeth onto the end of a branch above an abyss?"
"I'd go and pluck the one raspberry that I'd seen clinging to the cliff."

The koan and any other form of meditation also prepare you for Death. The koan is a short-circuiting that comes to no end. Death is always calculated into the sum of Life. Death burns up, consumes during Life, like a Persian who ate up, devoured a red pepper.

In the seventeenth century the Zen master Ingen arrived in Japan from China. He brought with him a great number of people skilled in sculpture, woodcarving, painting and other arts. With them he founded a new Zen sect, the Obaku. Ingen came with fresh ideas into a Japan that had been shutting itself off from the outside world for years. Thereby his sect, the smallest Zen sect, could exert a great influence not only on all areas of art, but also on everyday life. His arrival imparted a new stimulus to the spiritual and artistic climate of Japan at that time. Today it remains the sect wherein the greatest freedom and openness obtain. So it is no wonder that the photos of this book could be taken in a monastery of this very same Obaku sect.

Zen works creatively. Its influence on Western culture is owing to this. Our production-consumption society yearns for a justification that they cannot give themselves for it. Zen dropped into it with the writings of Daisetz T. Suzuki in the same way that Ingen arrived in Japan. Under his influence, especially on the West Coast of North America, various Zen groups have formed. It is chiefly young people who withdraw into them so as, through meditation and work, to give new meaning, to impart new 'sense' to life. It was chiefly the Beat Generation, with Jack Kerouac and Allen Ginsberg heading it, who found in Zen a doctrine that not only awakened in them an urge to roam their minds and the map, but also provided them with arguments against the rut-routine-drag of the materialistic consumption society into which they were born and which disgusted them. Their influence on young people, artists and laymen, has been immense; moreover they were supported in the field of scholarship by such people as Christmas Humphreys and Alan W. Watts, who both further amplified and propagated the statement of Buddhism for our Western world. Especially Alan Watts has come evermore to identify with the young; not only students, but youth in general. His influence is of inestimable value.

I've just spoken of Zen as a doctrine, but Zen is not a doctrine. A doctrine has an end; Zen never lets you rest, neither teaches nor reaches conclusions, ever keeping its coming to 'Sudden Awakening', going from standpoint to starting-point. Zen is quick. It has thereby also taken hold of our 'fast world'. Zen is good for all people because it isn't a doctrine, but a way of life, because it removes supposed uncertainties, because it clears out fixed opinions, because it brings you back to being 'un-signified'. If you want to keep an open eye on art, science and life, yes, if you want to bring these under a common denominator again, Zen can do it. Zen is not intellectual, but indeed intelligent. Zen says get rid of your ideas—live. If one gets carried away with the thesis that 'matter doesn't exist', Zen takes a stone and plunks it on your head. If however you have totally turned into stone, Zen says "matter doesn't exist." And that's why Zen can say: Freedom isn't doing what you like, but liking what you do. That's the road to 'liberation'. Or: If you want to be sure you're on the way, close your eyes and walk on. And if you want to see in the dark, blow out the candle. And if you're sitting, you are sitting; if you happen to be eating, you're eating and if you're asleep you're sleeping.
Zen is Alice in Wonderland. And even about Nirvana Zen can say:
One can call it neither empty nor not-empty
One, yet neither one
So as to point it out
We call it empty . . . .

BERT SCHIERBEEK

16

i do not know its name
a name for it is 'way'
pressed for designation
i call it great
great means outgoing
outgoing, far-reaching
far-reaching, return

Lao Tze

wake up

if you meet someone on the street
who's in possession of the truth
you may not speak to him
nor may you pass him by in silence
how do you want to meet him?
master Wu-men says:
if one meets the master of truth on the street
you mustn't step up to him
with either words or silence
the best thing to do
is smack him in the face
whoever wants to understand everything
must understand this too

got up
haven't eaten
stomach empty
fish awaits
stick lifted
wood on wood
day begins

the master

if you've a stick
i'll give you one
if you've no stick
i'll take it away

it all begins with a knock
on the fish
a sound
stomp on the ground
a sound

what, Toyo, is the sound
of one hand clapping?
Toyo pondered this for years
and said:
the sound of silence

where the master is, there is truth
respect for the master is respect for truth

Basho

now all eat together

even to the saucepan
wherein potatoes cook —
a moonlit night

Kyoroku

芋を煮る　鍋うちも

月夜かな

行六

because we are empty
we can give to eat

i am a person
who eats his breakfast
and looks into the morning glories

big clean-up
statues and Buddhas
go outside

who here is dusting off?
who's handling the broom?
if dust doesn't exist
nothing needs dusting

Else lifts the broom
Bert gets a coughing-fit
Else says—
if dust doesn't exist
then why are you coughing?

glistening clean
statues and Buddhas
inside again

Kyogen sweeps the floor

one strike made him forget
what he had learned
what kind of sound was it?
a piece of brick immediately
turned into gold

Zen monk Kyogen of China was a disciple of Isan.
He was fond of keeping notes of his masters and thought a
great deal about them.
One day, he found that all the notes and knowledge he had
accumulated were after all of no use in really understanding
Zen. He burned them, and being so disappointed at his
inability to gain satori, he decided to go on with his pursuit.
He retired to a country temple where he devoted himself to
looking after an old master's graveyard.
One day, while sweeping the ground, it happened that a
piece of stone swept away by his broom struck a bamboo
nearby.
The sound thus produced awakened his mind to a state of
enlightenment.
He composed a poem in which this "one strike" is referred to.

what is
the essence of
the Buddha?

dung

SHO SAI MYO KICHIJYO DHARANI

NO MO SAM MAN DA MOTO NAN OHA RA CHI KOTO SHA SONO
NAN TO JI TO EN GYA GYA GYA KI GYA KI UN NUN SHIFU
RA SHIFU RA HARA SHIFU RA HARA SHIFU RA CHISHU SA
CHISHU SA CHISHU RI CHISHU RI SOHA JA SOHA JA SEN CHI GYA
SHIRI E SOMO KO

namo-amida-butsu is inexhaustible
however often one repeats the name
it is inexhaustible
namo-amida-butsu
namo-amida-butsu

when you understand you belong to the family
when you do not understand you are a stranger
those who do not understand belong to the family
and when they understand they are strangers

sound comes to the ear
the ear goes to sound
when you blot out sound and sense
what do you understand?

while listening with ears
one never can understand
to understand intimately
one should see sound   Ekai

in the temple stand eighteen wooden figures
made in the Chinese Ming dynasty by a Chinese sculptor
who was requested by Ingen to come to Japan

a monk asked the master:
is there a doctrine
which no master has ever taught before?
yes
said the master
what then?
no mind
no Buddha
nothing

Nan-chuan declared
the way is no visible thing
nor is it an invisible thing
it is nothing knowable
don't look for it
don't teach it
don't name it
be as spacious and open as the sky
and you are on the way

one minute of sitting, one inch of Buddha
like lightning all thoughts come and pass
just once look into your mind-depths
nothing else has ever been

Manzan

Gau-fung asked his pupils
all things return to the One
to where does the One return?

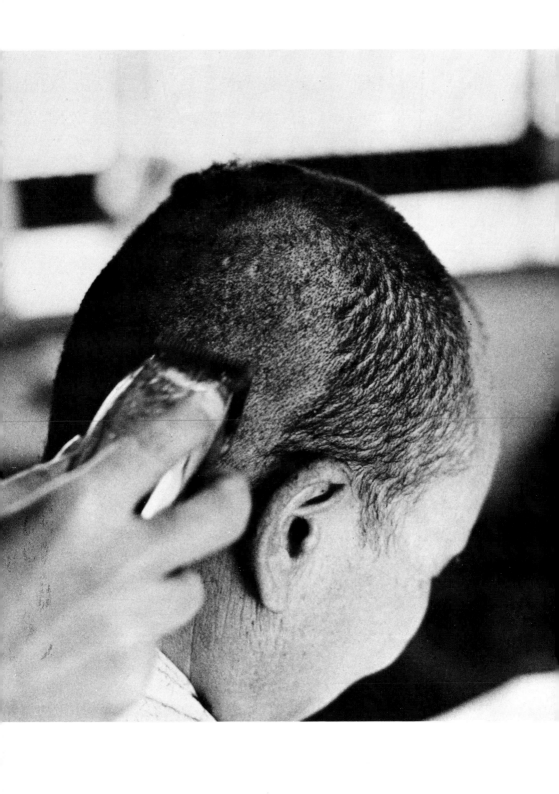

lectric
Zen
ceremonial

BIBASHI-BUTSU DAIOSHO SHIKI-BUTSU DAIOSHO BISHAFU-BUTSU DAIO
TSU DAIOSHO SHAKAMUNI-BUTSU DAIOSHO MAKAKASHO DAIOSHO AN
IOSHO MISHAKA DAIOSHO VASHUMITSU DAIOSHO BUTSUDANANDAI DA
NABOTEI DAIOSHO KABIMARA DAIOSHO NAGYAHARAJUNA DAIOSHO I
SHATA DAIOSHO KUMORATA DAIOSHO SHAYATA DAIOSHO VASHUBAN
OSHO BASHASHITA DAIOSHO FUNYOMITTA DAIOSHO HANNYATARA DA
SHO DAI-I DOSHIN DAIOSHO DAIMAN KONIN DAIOSHO DAIKAN ENO DA
IOSHO UNGAN DONJO DAIOSHO TOZAN RYOKAI DAIOSHO UNGODOYC

KURUSON-BUTSU DAIOSHO KUNAGONMUNI-BUTSU DAIOSHO KASHO-BU

DAIOSHO SHONAWASHU DAIOSHO UBAKIKUTA DAIOSHO DAITAKA DA

O FUDAMITTA DAIOSHO BARISHIBA DAIOSHO FUNAYASHA DAIOSHO A

DAIBA DAIOSHO RAGORATA DAIOSHO SOGYANANDAI DAIOSHO KAYA

AIOSHO MANURA DAIOSHO KAKUROKUNA DAIOSHO SHISHIBODAI DAI

O BODAIDARUMA DAIOSHO TAISO EKA DAIOSHO KANCHI SOSAN DAIO

O SEIGEN GYOSHI DAIOSHO SEKITO KISEN DAIOSHO YAKUSAN IGEN DA

OSHO DOAN DOHI DAIOSHO DOAN KANSHI DAIOSHO RYOZAN ENKAN

Shogen asked
why does the enlightened man not stand up
on his feet and explain himself?
and he also said
it is not necessary for speech
to come from the tongue

Mumon's comment:
Shogen spoke plainly enough, but how many will understand?
if anyone comprehends, he should come to my place
and test out my big stick
why look here?
to test real gold you must see through fire

if the feet of enlightenment moved,
the great ocean would overflow
if the head bowed, it would look down upon the heavens
such a body has no place to rest . . .
let another continue this poem

with eyes closed
i see my inner being in detail
thus i see my true nature

One of the monks apparently felt that his concentration
had fallen off and asked to be stricken with the stick.
The Jikido, the priest who walks back and forth with
the Kyosaku, dealt the strikes of the stick out to him.
Then some more bowing.

with this staff in my hand
i measure the deep and the undeep
the staff supports the heavens
and makes firm the earth

Basho

six hours Zazen per day

Zazen

Zen sitting is the way of perfect tranquility
inwardly not a shadow of perception
outwardly not a shade of difference between phenomena
identified with yourself
you no longer think
nor do you seek enlightenment of the mind
or disburdenment of illusions
you are a flying bird with no mind to twitter
a mountain unconscious of other mountains

Meiho

Kokai's Satori poem

taking hold   one is lost in nothingness   letting go   the origin's regained   the music stoppe

shadow's touched   my door   again the village moon's above the river

the doors of my day-room

Friday

Got up at five this morning to the high-toned sounding of the gong and the dull thumping of the wooden fish, the kaipan, a kind of temple bell used for announcing the hours of the day.

This morning was a cold one. My first night in a Japanese bed, consisting of a thick blanket with a spread over it, was very comfortable. Then this bed itself lies on a thick mat, the tatami, It was quarter after five and still dark. From somewhere around me I heard the sound of a priest clearing his throat, which was rather frightening. The first day at Mampukuji had begun.

I had to hurry to be on time for the service held in the temple, beginning at five-thirty. A nearly superhuman quiet prevailed in the garden surrounding the temple building. I stood waiting until the monks arrived, seven in all. The temple looks less sober than expected. There is a good deal of gold and there are some large colored vases and artificial flowers. A dazzling light shining on the altar displays a strange shadow show. The service in the temple is much different than I had imagined. Actually, at first glance it much resembles a Catholic service. Sutras are sung in a ceremony of continual standing and sitting. Every now and then there is the jingling of little bells and the sound of a gong. I had imagined the service would be much simpler, without pomp and circumstance, though sound and motion do have symbolic significance. The service lasted half an hour.

Meanwhile it had gotten lighter outside. The monks went to the Zendo, the hall where Zazen is held. I went to the other Zendo, the one used for visitors and guests who want to do some Zazen. With special slippers on, held in place by a strip between the big toe and the other toes, I stepped into the Zendo, left foot forward, to the left side of the entrance. Because it was so cold I had kept on my sox, so I couldn't walk so easily in those slippers. Two Japanese men were standing there waiting for me. It was to be the first time I would be doing Zazen under the instruction of a Zen master. I had to be seated on two white cushions, in a sort of tailor's posture. The two others were at once sitting in the lotus posture. During the Zazen, the sitting in meditation, I held my hands in a special position, with the left palm turned out, laying on the inside of the right hand with the tips of the thumbs up against each other. I was absolutely not allowed to move; the object was to get the mind as empty as possible. The eyes were half closed, although one was able to see. After a short time I got dizzy and was afraid I'd fall down. Luckily I had read in one of the instruction books of the Soto sect that in a case like this one should concentrate upon the forehead. Often I could catch myself thinking from one subject to another. The master rang the bell twice and my first Zazen session was over. I was allowed to stretch my legs for a moment and then we remained sitting in Zazen for a half hour more. My back began to hurt and my hands dropped out of the proper position. I wondered how the monks can keep this up for six hours a day.

Saturday

Only through having first seen quite a variety of Zen gardens did I come to fully appreciate the gardens here at Mampukuji. They are very simple and not especially beautiful, but they provide an enormous quietude. The temple buildings and the gardens go together, they are attuned to each other. There are galleries running from one building to the other, with gardens on each side. These are gardens to look at, not to walk through. How do they get these patterns? Probably with a kind of iron rake.

Today I went to see the monks having breakfast. They sing monotonous sutras before they start. The breakfast consisted of a bowl of cold rice and some green tea; for me too. No talking is allowed during the mealtime. I even eat separately, right next to the kitchen, where also other visitors eat, and now and then a priest as well. Fortunately I am able to get on well with the chopsticks. The conversation at table is small talk. Although one of the priests speaks a few words of English, the rest speak only Japanese, which I speak very brokenly, and with my little English-Japanese phrase-book I amazingly get on rather well.

Sunday

The special service in the temple today was very impressive. The head-priest was dressed in a purple robe and the initiation ceremony was celebrated for about 15 women, all dressed in beautiful kimonos, who were graduated as mistress in ikebana, *the Japanese art of flower-arrangement.*

This evening I've been doing a lot of Zazen; this time for about an hour-and-a-half. One of my fellow zazen-sitters got hit three times on his back with the kyosaku, *a long, flat stick. First he was tapped upon his right shoulder and then he bowed down with both hands pressed flat together; and then he completely prostrated himself, so he was open to receive the straight strikes of the stick on the flat of his back. One asks for these strokes with the stick if one feels that one hasn't been concentrating well enough, or one gets them from the master for the same reason. After this ritual he again bowed down and resumed his former Zazen-posture. I had completely lost my concentration and was afraid that I, too, would get a beating. But I was to be spared this treatment, perhaps because I was still a beginner, and a woman, and . . . a westerner.*

Monday

    If I've understood it properly, the monks have their heads shaved every Monday. I am quite surprised to find it is done with an electric shaver. One definitely feels the effect of the modern Western society again in contrast to the old Japanese tradition. Sometimes I feel like I'm living a few centuries ago in that I'm not having any contact with the outside world. After the hustle and bustle of Tokyo, this is a wonderful place to come to be, and I already feel more relaxed. Could this be from the Zazen?

    I'm still hoping to get to photograph the monks doing Zazen, but it seems that they aren't going to let me in to the holy Zendo.

    Lunch and supper are excellent. I eat out of three little red bowls, which fit into each other and into which a small napkin is placed to clean them. All these are wrapped up in a serviette, between which the chopsticks are put. The biggest bowl is for the rice, the second for soup and the sauce, and the third little bowl is for tea. The meal is vegetarian, no fish or meat, but a lot of fresh vegetables and fruit. To the amazement of the priests, I am able to get along fine with this diet, though I wonder how long I can keep this up. Mampukuji is famous for this food, called Fucha Ryori, or 'food of the priests'. It was brought over to Japan from China by Ingen in the seventeenth century and its ingredients have remained unaltered to this day, although there have been a few small adaptations made to suit the Japanese table. The Japanese people love it. There are also a lot of restaurants where one can get this food, but for the authentic old-time diet one goes to eat at Mampukuji. They have a special kitchen for it there.

Tuesday

Tonight I have to think about what master Dogen, the founder of the Soto sect in Japan, had so clearly formulated seven centuries ago: To study Buddhism is to study the self. To study the self is to be enlightened by all things. To be enlightened by all things is to be free from attachment to the body and mind of one's self and other's selves. There it stands so clear and simple, but it is so difficult for our 'logical' Western mind and manner of thinking. Every day I have tried to explain that I'd like so much to see the raking of the gardens. Today at last it has been arranged. An old priest, whom I hadn't seen as yet, was busy sweeping up. With a great deal of effort I brought him to understand what I wanted, whereupon he promptly went to get a massive nine-toothed rake. He explained to me that he was already 83 years old. I was afraid that the work would be too heavy for him with the dragging of that monster rake through the mixture of sand and gravel. But he plowed through it with a grin.

Almost all Zen masters whom I have met seem to have a tremendous sense of humor and they often have a fun-filled gleam in their eyes with laughing wrinkles around them.

Today the monks are busy with the 'Big Clean-up'. They walk around in a sort of physical training outfit with a white towel around their heads and carry around mops and big buckets of water. The various altars get cleaned, the statues are taken down. In retrospect, they seem to do this every day, not only to clean them off, but also for the physical work to stimulate the circulation of blood.

Wednesday

Today I've come to know more about the history of Mampukuji temple. This is the main temple of the OBAKU sect, one of the three Zen sects in Japan, that controls about 500 temples. This sect is the latest one to be introduced into Japan, in 1654, when the Chinese priest, Ingen, came to Japan, bringing along with him various artists and artisans. Mampukuji's architecture has a distinctly Chinese character, which is most noticeable in the white walls with the round portals. It is said that some of the wood used for the temple comes from Holland. The Dutchmen intended to use it to build a fort on Taiwan. By cause of shipwreck it appears to have been washed ashore in Japan and to have come into the hands of Ingen and his companions. Up to the eighteenth century there had continually been Chinese priests in this sect, but now it is being run entirely by Japanese priests. The main temple and the monastery sustain themselves from the gifts of believers and by the contributions of other temples. Every now and then Mampukuji gets visited by tourists, and the student monks have the task of guiding them around. An admission price is levied and this too is a source of income for the temple.

To my utter astonishment this morning a group of men dressed in some sort of grey uniform marched into the temple. It seems that they were employees of a chemical factory. They were sent here for two days to do Zazen, to resort to a sort of retreat. In the evening they were coming to the same hall in which I was doing Zazen. I found it unsettling to see them all getting hit with the stick and I really thought that soon it would get around to me, but luckily it didn't. These were men of various ages and in spite of that they all could sit in the lotus posture very easily. Will I ever get that far?

Thursday

The chief priest and other priests are geting to be more and more friendly to me, and it seems as if they are getting to appreciate me in a certain way, and slowly-but-surely they are giving me more and more privileges so that I can look at and photograph the life of the monks. Probably they are surprised that I go on with the life here with its strict rules and totally different living-habits. The food for lunch and supper is especially good, but breakfast sometimes felt a little heavy. Last night one of the priests invited me over for breakfast. He is the only one who is married, and his wife seems to be an uncomplicated little woman who is very friendly. They live in a room with Japanese windows of rice paper, of which a few of the panes are ripped. We sat on the floor with our legs under the low table under which a built-in electric stove was burning. A kind of thick tablecloth spread across the table hung to the floor, so we could keep our legs warm. This was the only furniture in the room and further than that there was no heating. They had brought bread (pan *in Japanese*) especially for me, and there was also some coffee. After a week that really tasted fine. The Japanese are wonderful hosts.

Tomorrow is my last day at the temple and I try once more to make clear to this priest Kusunoki that I really do hope to get to photograph the monks at their Zazen.

Friday:

This morning my thoughts during the Zazen were so much on the Zazen the monks were doing that I couldn't concentrate. Fortunately Kusunoki was to help me out. After breakfast he went with me to the monk's Zendo. It was very dark there. The monks, in Zazen, were all sitting in a row, with the master sitting separately upon a chair. I got a signal that I could now start with the picture taking. I felt that my being there was almost too much and with the shutter making a lot of noise in these super-silent spaces. One of the monks apparently felt that his concentration was falling off, probably due to my presence, and asked to be hit with the stick. The 'Jikido', the priest, who was walking back and forth with the kyosaku, administered the stickbeating to him. I was taking pictures all the while and made use of this unique opportunity. Then the bowing again. I was afraid that they'd call me back. After about ten minutes I had to stop and with a timid "domo arigato," thank you very much, and a deep bow, I left the Zendo. My mission—to let Zen enter the lens as the light of life filling the Void—was now completed.

Else Madelon Hooykaas, Nov. 1970, Mampukuji Temple, Kyoto

the master creates order in disorder
and perfection in imperfection
as his garden is there as well as not
the garden and non-garden is another garden

the master is raking the sand
in his garden
with a nine-toothed fork
here he's raking straight lines
but he can also rake
rivers and waterfalls in the sand
bubbling brooks and the surging surf
in which he places rocks as mountains
or sometimes throws up
as ship-shaped formations
and scales Nature down or up
into the dimensions of his garden
and the garden he rakes is to be his garden
his design
and it always shall be
it shall not be a garden in which to walk
but a garden to see
for it is the downbeat of his meditation
and shall convey this to others
he will give it a name such as
the mountain of eternal youth
or the garden of tranquil sleep

the monk said
this stone
thus this ship
is sailing downstream
and see the turtle
swimming against the current

ending life means not dying
not dying means ending life
ending life means
becoming Namo-amida-butsu

this garden is structured in a way that whoever removes bu

even as he'd spoil a musical compositio

ne stone from its place destroys the harmony of the structure

y the removal of one note

the way is void

used
but never full
it is an abyss
like a forefather
from which all things come

Lao-tse

do you hear the rushing of the river
yes master
if so
that is the way

this is Ginkaku-ji, that is, the 'silver temple' in Kyoto

this is the main temple, Mampukuji

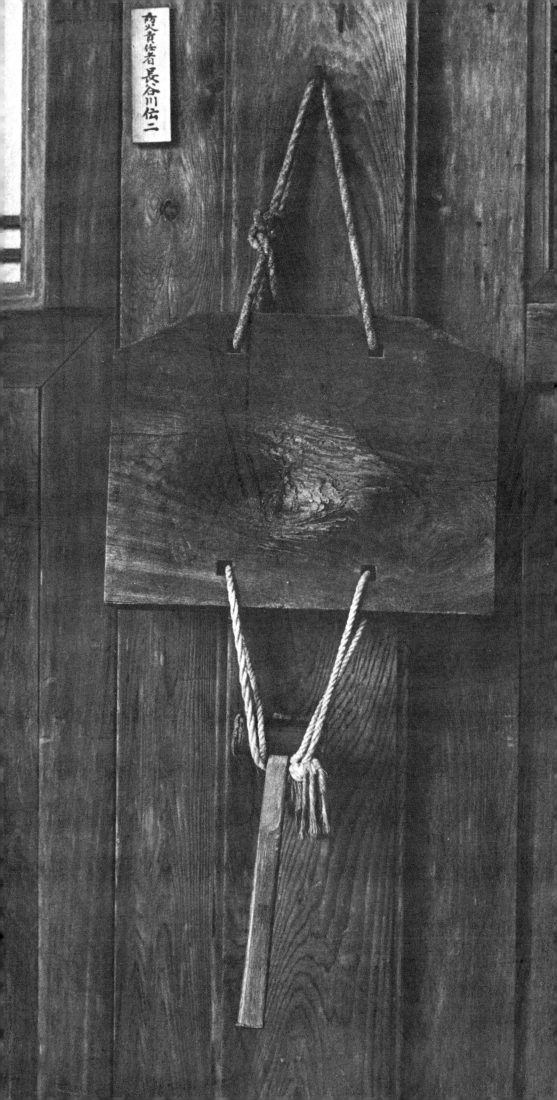

at the entrance to the Zendo hangs this wooden plaque
about which is written this Chinese poem

the world is transitory
and all experience quickly passes
each of us must wake up from his dream
there is no time to lose

This garden was designed by Soam, a famous garden architect.
It is somewhat elevated from the surrounding grounds.
The garden is called "the Sea of Silver Sand," the Ginshadan.
Its form is borrowed from the form of a lake in China.
The furrows in the sand are ripples wherein the moonlight
is mirrored, thus illuminating the garden at night.
The hill in the form of Mount Fuji is called Kogetsudai.
Shogun Yoshimasa, the priest who built this temple in 1482,
used to enjoy looking at the moon from this point.

shing trees

all people have wishes, which are written
on wrappers of a kind of taffy
you can buy in the temple
if you want your wish to come true
you hang this piece of taffy on a little tree
and as there are many people with wishes
the trees fill up and finally the fulfilled wishes
drop from the trees
and along comes the monk
and sweeps up the wishes

The dry gardens are gardens without water wherein the portions
where water would be are represented by stone and sand
Therefore the name dry garden or rock garden.
This technique in stone and sand is comparable
to the black and white ink-drawings.

only genuine awakening results in that
only fools seek sainthood for reward
lifting a hand
the stone lantern announces daybreak
smiling, the void nods its enormous head

Nensho

Cha no Yu

The four features of the tea-ceremony are harmony, respect,
purity and peace.
That is, the pouring of the water, the simmering song of the kettle,
the simplicity and neatness, the holding on to and delightful regard
of the cup, and then the bitter taste of the tea.
The guest's respect for one another and for the tea-mistress,
all this together is a form of meditation, a single long on-going
ceremony within which all is One.
The tea-ceremony is no mere taking of tea.
This kind of ceremony requires that the house be cleaned up,
the garden raked down, in short, that everything be done for the
reception of the guests.
When the latter arrive they are received in a separate waiting-room,
from which via a short garden-path and low door they enter
the tea-room for the ceremony.
This room measures four and one-half tatamis of floor-space.
A tatami is a mat of 180 by 80 cm.

at first the way of tea was faceless
diligence and mastery were the only laws
but rules or no
one merely need give up his will

and full of wonder the world takes on a new face

ikebana

ikebana means living flower
it is the name of the art of flower arrangement
every young girl in Japan learns it before she marries
according to the rules of tradition
flower arrangement is a world of grace cultivated in the world of nature
Ten-shi-jin, heaven, earth and people, are brought together
in an asymmetrical unity with the arrangement of twig, leaf and flower

in this tea-room on this occasion there is a brush-drawn haiku
and the ikebana which are to be admired by the guests
and one experiences this together as one
peace comes to us out of nature and we restore it to nature

if Zen would seem to have no place in our generation
then Zen is dealing with a lot of troubled situations

if you try to keep the gate and doors of a collapsing house
standing up, then too you're in for a heap of trouble

ZEN

NOW

the stream congealed in sand and pebbles
the eye reposes on the flow
the sand the pebbles
streams emptiness
and seeing the landscape
makes multiples
to its own blindness

Kyu-do

the art of archery

for them the contest consists in the archer
aiming at himself and yet not at himself
in hitting himself and yet not himself
and thus becoming simultaneously aimer and aim, hitter and hit
it is necessary for the archer to become
in spite of himself an unmoved center
then comes the supreme and ultimate miracle
the art becomes artless
the shooting becomes not shooting
a shooting without bow and arrow
the teacher becomes a pupil again
the master a beginner
the end a beginning
and the beginning a perfection

how can the shot actually be let fly
if i don't shoot it?
it shoots

archer arrow bow distance and target are one